money matters

Sean Callery

QEB

QEB Publishing

Editor: Sarah Eason
Designer: Calcium
Picture Researcher: Maria Joannou

Published in the United States in 2010 by
QEB Publishing, Inc.
3 Wrigley, Suite A
Irvine, CA 92618

www.qed-publishing.co.uk

Library of Congress Cataloging-in-Publication Data

Callery, Sean.
  QEB money matters / Sean Callery.
      p. cm.
  Includes bibliographical references and index.
  ISBN 978-1-59566-729-8 (library binding)
  1. Money--Juvenile literature. I. Title. II. Title: Money matters.
  HG221.5.C25 2011
  332.4--dc22
                                    2010001156

Printed in China

Picture credits
Key: t = top, b = bottom, c = center, l = left, r = right

Alamy Images: Asia-pix 23t, Best View Stock 13b, Jeff Greenberg 33b, Ivy Close Images 16, Ben Molyneux
People 48, Rolf Richardson 21t; **Corbis:** Annika Erickson/Blend Images 43t, Hoberman Collection 11c, Tetra
Images 3br, Sandro Vannini 27t, Naashon Zalk 31t; **Getty Images:** Absodels 34, Bloomberg 10b, The Bridgeman
Art Library/James Edwin McConnell 19tr, The Image bank/Ron Levine 26, Superstock 40; **Istockphoto:**
Ranplett 43b; **Photolibrary:** Imagebroker.net/KFS KFS 8b; **Rex Features:** EDPpics/Butcher 30, Anthony Upton
41t; **Science Photo Library:** Aandrew Brookes, National Physical Laboratory 41b; **Shutterstock:** Andresr 38,
Utekhina Anna 37b, Sue Ashe 17t, AXL 7t, Geanina Bechea 1, 29b, Joe Belanger 18t, Dallas Events Inc 3tr, 15tr,
Dennizn 14b, Elena Elisseeva 39t, Marty Ellis 25t, EML 29t, ER__09 45t, Sonya Etchison 25b, Mike Flippo 5b,
Tomislav Forgo 3l, 9t, Hank Frentz 19b, Gelpi 24, Giuseppe__R 18b, 47, Mandy Godbehear 42, Christopher Hall
37tl, Heizel 9b, J. Helgason 5t, Horst Kanzek 15b, Kinetic Imagery 35b, 39bl, 39br, Georgios Kollidas 35tc, 35tr,
Marekuliasz 15tl, Jo Mikus 22b, Monkey Business Images 23b, 37tr, Myotis 19tl, Nattika 22t, Andrei Nekrassov
11b, Oleksandr 17b, Ostromec 21b, Losevsky Pavel 32, 33t, Photobank 6, Todd Pierson 44, Pjmorley 36, Tatiana
Popova 13t, Rossario 4, Satyrja 8t, Vladimir Sazonov 14t, S__E 28, Russell Shively 20t, Christi Tolbert 45b,
Suzanne Tucker 31b, Stephen VanHorn 35tl, Kachalkina Veronika 27b, Keith Wheatley 12, Feng Yu 17c; **Topham
Picturepoint:** The Granger Collection 7b, 10t; **Wikimedia Commons:** Marie-Lan Nguyen 11t

CONTENTS

WHAT IS MONEY?

Money is the coins, notes, cards, and checks that we use to pay for things.

We need money

Almost all the things that we need to live cost money. We pay money for our food, shelter, and clothes.

We need money to build things such as playgrounds.

What is it worth?

Which of your toys do you like best? The person who made it was paid money for their work. The person who sold the toy was paid money, too. The person who bought the toy had to pay for it. Your toy is worth money.

This teddy bear costs money.

A receipt shows what you paid for.

Money talk

Look at the receipt you get when you shop in a food store. This is the long piece of paper that shows the cost of everything you have bought. Which item cost the most? Which cost the least?

BEFORE MONEY

In the days before money, people swapped things.

Swap shop

People swapped things they already had for things they needed. They could have swapped some fish for a loaf of bread. They could have swapped some cows for a place to live. This is called barter.

In some places, people still barter.

How much is it worth?

Imagine you have a truck or a doll, and you want your friend's cards. You can offer to swap them. How many cards is your toy worth: one, ten, or more? The amount depends on how much your friend wants your toy!

What would you swap for this truck?

In the story of "Jack and the Beanstalk," Jack swaps his cow for some magic beans.

Money talk

Do you collect stickers or cards? How many would you swap for a candy bar?

SHELLS AND FEATHERS

Some strange things were used as money before coins and bills were invented.

The people on one island in the Pacific Ocean used red feathers as money!

Let's trade!

If people could not barter goods, they traded with objects that they valued. People used different objects depending on where they lived. For example, in China they used cowrie shells as money. In ancient Rome, they used salt.

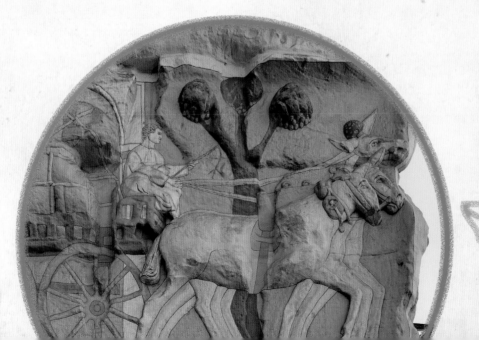

People used to travel a long way to trade.

First coins

The first known metal coins were used in China hundreds of years ago. The coins were made of a metal called bronze. Later, other people started to use valuable metals such as gold, silver, and copper as money.

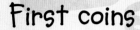

Metals, such as gold, can be shaped into blocks.

MONEY MATH

Be a Chinese trader. You have 10 cowrie shells. What can you buy from this list?

bag of rice	5 shells
egg	1 shell
bag of coffee	4 shells
chicken	3 shells

What could you buy with a cowrie shell?

USING COINS

Coins are pieces of metal that are marked to show that they are money.

Stamp it!

The first flat coins were made in Turkey. They were made by hand, and stamped on one side with a picture of a lion.

Stamping coins with an image is called minting.

MAD MONEY FACT

Coins are made at factories called mints. The U.S. Mint in Philadelphia can make one million coins in 30 minutes. It is the biggest mint in the world.

Goddess and owl

Ancient Greek coins were made of silver. They had a picture of Athena, the goddess of war, on one side. On the other side was an owl, which was a sign of wisdom.

This ancient Greek coin shows the goddess Athena.

Use your head

The first living person to have their portrait on a coin was the Roman emperor, or ruler, Julius Caesar.

Caesar put his picture on a coin to show how important he was.

HOW COINS CHANGED

Coins had to be made carefully, so that people could not copy them to make their own money.

Cut it out!

Sometimes dishonest people cut bits of metal off the coins before they spent them. They melted these bits into one piece of metal, and sold it. To stop this, coinmakers began to put ridges around the edges of coins.

If an ancient coin had a smooth edge, this meant part of the coin had been cut off.

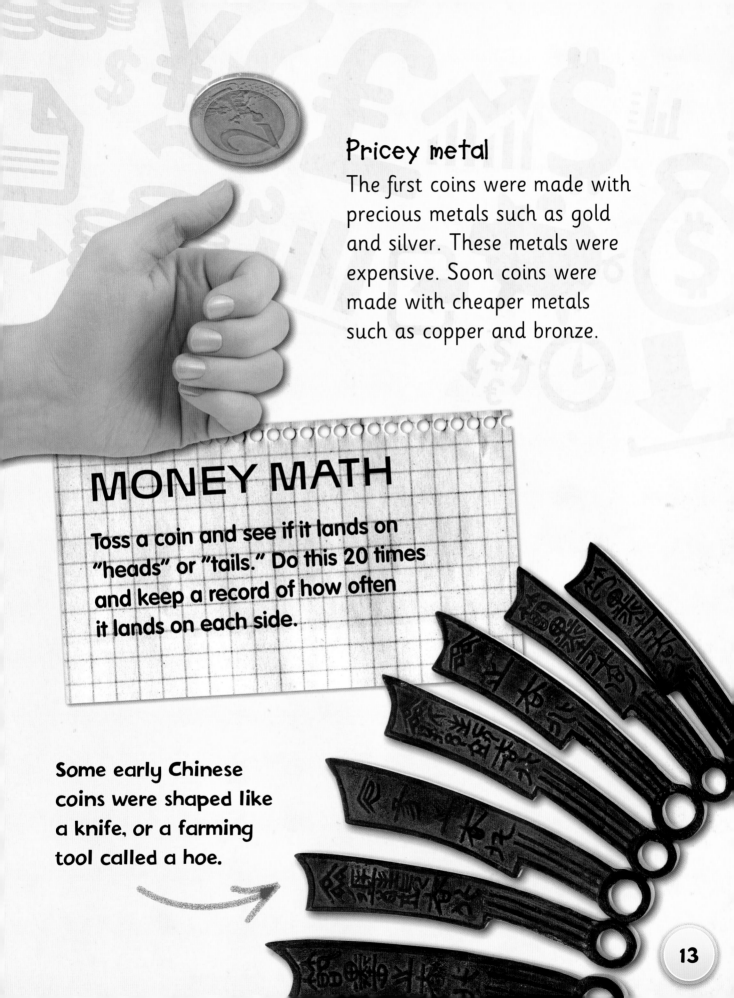

Pricey metal

The first coins were made with precious metals such as gold and silver. These metals were expensive. Soon coins were made with cheaper metals such as copper and bronze.

MONEY MATH

Toss a coin and see if it lands on "heads" or "tails." Do this 20 times and keep a record of how often it lands on each side.

Some early Chinese coins were shaped like a knife, or a farming tool called a hoe.

SHAPES AND SIZES

Coins today come in many sizes, and not all are round.

Bags of money

You need to be able to see quickly which coins are in your purse, so they need to be lots of different sizes and different shapes.

In Canada, the one-dollar coin has eleven sides.

How many sides?

In the United States, all the coins are round, but they are different sizes. In Australia, the 50 cent coin has twelve sides.

These early Chinese coins have a hole in the middle.

String it!

Some early coins had a hole in the middle. This was so that they could be hung together on strings.

MAD MONEY FACT!

The Penny Farthing bicycle was named after two British coins—a penny and a farthing. The bike's big wheel is big like a penny and the small wheel is little, like a farthing.

USING PAPER

Coins are expensive to make and heavy to carry around. Paper money was invented because it is cheaper to make and is light to carry.

Paper tale

The Chinese were the first to make bills, hundreds of years ago. The first paper bills in Europe and the United States were used about 400 years ago.

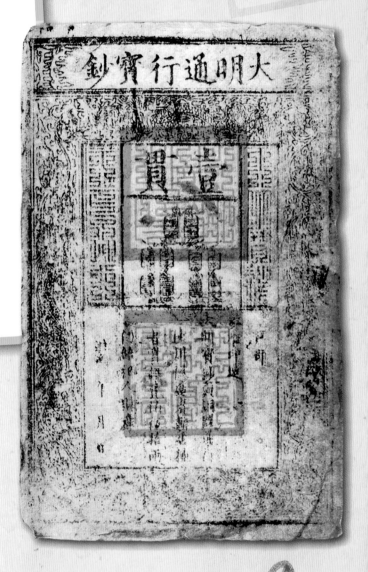

The Chinese made the first paper money.

Money was once made from tobacco leaves.

Not just paper

Bills have been made from all sorts of materials, including tobacco leaves, leather, silk, and seal skin. Today they are made from strong paper that will last a long time.

100 dollar bills are not used as much as 1 dollar bills so they last longer!

MAD MONEY FACT!

Bills today have many special markings on them, to make them difficult to copy.

COUNT IT!

Fingers and thumbs

There are 100 cents in a U.S. dollar and 100 pence in a U.K. pound. You may find it easiest to count in tens because you can use the ten digits (fingers and thumbs) on your hands.

Most modern money is decimal, which means it can be counted in tens and hundreds.

Two thumbs and eight fingers make ten digits.

Money ahoy!

Pirates counted their coins in eights rather than tens. They used a Spanish coin called the "peso." It could be split into eight pieces, each worth a "reale."

In pirate stories, pesos are called "pieces of eight."

Going decimal

In the 1700s, Thomas Jefferson (who later became President) suggested a decimal money system. There were no decimal coins in use until 1792.

MAD MONEY FACT!

Pirates were paid "danger money." If a pirate lost a leg or an arm in battle, he was paid 800 pieces of eight by his captain!

This old coin is a British shilling. Shillings are no longer in use.

AROUND THE WORLD

There are about 180 currencies, or types of money, in the world.

Shop abroad

Some countries share a currency. Other countries want to have their own currency. When you visit a country you must buy some of their money to spend there.

The table shows some important currencies and their signs.

COUNTRY	CURRENCY	SIGN
Australia	Australian dollar	$
Brazil	real	R$
Canada	Canadian dollar	$
China	yuan	CNY
Europe	Euro	€
India	rupee	Rs
Japan	yen	¥
South Africa	rand	R
United Kingdom	pound	£
United States	US dollar	$

New money

In 2002, sixteen countries in Europe gave up their old currencies and changed to one new currency, called the Euro.

These people are changing their money into another currency.

After the U.S. dollar, the Euro currency is used more than any other currency in the world.

A WORLD MARKET

People once had to meet to trade. Now they can do it on the phone, or by computer.

One world

We buy things from all around the world. The labels on your clothes and food show where they come from. The whole world is a marketplace now.

Some countries sell the bananas and sugar they grow to other countries that can't grow them.

Up and down

Prices of goods go up and down. If there is a lot of something for sale, it will be cheaper to buy. If there is less of something for sale, it is more expensive.

If there is not much coffee in the world, it will be expensive to buy.

MAD MONEY FACT!

Some people have a job buying and selling huge amounts of goods in the worldwide market. They use computers and telephones to do it.

Buy and sell

The price of something also goes up if a lot of people want to buy it. It goes down when fewer people want to buy it. This is called "supply and demand."

MAKING MONEY

Most people earn money by doing a job. They might make something, or do a service for someone else.

Jobs for adults

Adults do lots of different jobs. Some people make things, such as cars or computers. Others, such as farmers, grow food. Some, such as teachers and doctors, help people.

Doctors are paid to help people.

What are wages?

Anyone who does a job is paid money. This money is sometimes called a wage. Jobs that use more skills usually pay more money.

Skilled sportspeople can earn a lot of money.

Jobs for children

Older children can earn some money by doing jobs such as delivering newspapers or childminding.

Money talk

What job would you like to do? How much do you think you should be paid for it?

Maybe you could earn money by walking a dog?

PAYING TAX

Everyone who earns money pays some of their wages to the government. This money is called tax. Governments use taxes to pay for running the country.

Money for everyone

Taxes pay for services that are used by everyone, such as roads, schools, and hospitals. Taxes are not taken only from wages. When you buy things in a store, part of the price you pay is a tax that is paid to the government.

Taxes help to pay for museums.

Early tax

The first taxes were paid in ancient Egypt, thousands of years ago. Farmers had to give a share of their crops to the pharaoh, or ruler.

In ancient Egypt, tax was paid in grain instead of money.

MAD MONEY FACT!

The Aztecs made their enemies pay taxes in cocoa beans, which they made into chocolate.

Danger money

Another tax from long ago was called danegeld. People in Britain paid it to invaders from abroad called Vikings, so they would not attack their lands.

Vikings were given money so they would not rob local people.

SAVE IT!

What would you really like to buy? If it costs a lot, you might have to save up for it.

It can cost a lot of money to fix a damaged car.

Why save?
We save up for things we cannot afford to buy right now. Adults often save money to be able to pay an unexpected cost, such as repairs to a car.

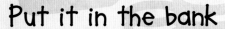

Put it in the bank

People who are saving money often put it in a bank to keep it safe. Banks can make people's money increase. This means they add a little bit extra to the money. Banks pay interest to savers.

You can take out your savings from an ATM, or cash machine.

MAD MONEY FACT!

A piggy bank is named after "pygg," a clay that was once used to make pots. People put money in a clay pot, and later broke it open to spend the money they had saved.

MONEY HELPS

You can use money to help those who are less fortunate than you.

Give, give, give

Sharing money means giving it to a charity or spending it on someone else. You could give money to someone who is doing a run or bike ride to raise money for a good cause.

These children dyed their hair or shaved their head to raise money!

Helping others

Business executive Bill Gates earned a lot of money out of making and selling computer products. He gives a lot of his money to help people around the world.

Bill Gates gives money to help others, especially children who are sick.

Money talk

If you had money to give to a charity, which one would you choose? Why?

You could do a sponsored bike ride or fun run to raise money for charity.

SPEND IT!

We spend money on things we need or want.

It's fun!
Spending money can be fun. You can buy something you need, such as a drink or a new pair of sneakers. Or you can spend your money on something you want, such as a new toy or a treat.

Money talk

Think of something you need and something you want. Which would you buy first? Why?

Choosing new toys can be fun!

Money left over

Adults spend most of their money on things they need such as a home, food, and clothes. With any money left over they may buy things they want, such as movie tickets or a vacation.

Everybody has to buy food.

What did you buy?

ALL CHANGE

Change is money
you get back
when you pay
with bills and coins.

**We call
bills and
coins "cash."**

Money back

You may not always have exactly the right money to pay for something. If you give coins or bills worth more, the store gives you some money back.

Work it out

Max lives in France. He buys a cereal bar worth 17 cents and hands over 20 cents. He is given 3 cents back, because he paid 3 cents too much. The 3 cents is his change.

You can collect loose change in a jar.

Loose coins

We also use the word "change" to mean a few loose coins. Some people collect their coins until they have a large amount.

MONEY MATH

You buy candy that costs 6 cents. You hand over 10 cents, or a dime. How much change will you get back?

WAYS TO PAY

Promise to pay

Cash pays for something on the spot. If we have money in a checking account, the bank gives us a book of checks. A check is a piece of paper that promises that the bank will pay money out of our account.

We can pay for things with cash, a paper check, or a plastic card.

Checks must be signed by the person who owns them.

Pay by plastic

We can also use plastic cards to buy things. We use cards to spend money from our checking account. When we pay with a card, we give a secret number called a PIN number. Every person has a different PIN number.

CREDIT CARD

0456 7890 1230 0456

EXPIRES 00/00

NAME MR A N OTHER

When someone uses their PIN number, it tells the bank they own the card and it is okay to take money from their account.

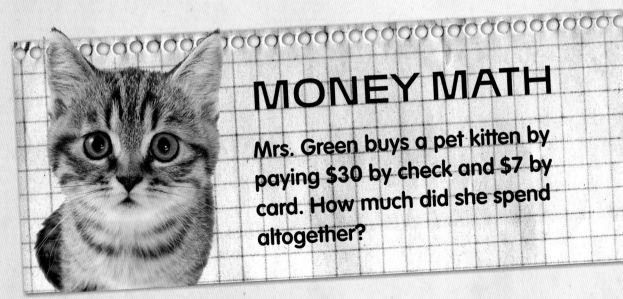

MONEY MATH

Mrs. Green buys a pet kitten by paying $30 by check and $7 by card. How much did she spend altogether?

HAVE A PLAN

Most people cannot buy what they want all the time. We have to plan how to spend our money.

Managing

The best way to manage money is to make a budget. This is a plan of the money you get in, called income, and the money you have to pay out, called expenses.

A budget shows if you can afford to buy something, such as a new car.

Spend or save?

If your expenses are more than your income, you have to find ways to spend less.

If you have more income than expenses, you can spend or save some money.

May	In	Out		Total
				$55
7th	$10	Dress $12		$43
10th				$53
14th	$10	CD $8		$45
15th				$55
21st	$10			

Money talk

Spend or save? Use two jars to find out! In one jar put money you can spend now. In a second jar put money you need to save to buy something. Which one has more money?

NOW

LATER

IN THE FUTURE

In the future, using cash and checks to pay for things will seem as out of date as paying with seashells.

No more cash

Today, people's wages are often paid straight into their checking account. Money can be taken or given through computers. Few people are still paid in cash.

In the past, workers received their pay in cash at the end of each week.

Going online

Today we can buy things on the Internet, or "online." We can also look at our checking accounts online. We will use this way of managing money more in the future.

Ticket to ride

Today we can pay for things such as train journeys with a special prepaid card or ticket. Money is paid into the card account before people travel.

In Britain, people who travel in London use a prepaid Oyster card instead of buying a paper ticket.

MAD MONEY FACT!

One day we might be able to pay just by having our fingerprints or our eyes scanned.

EARN IT!

Most people get their money by working to earn it. Children can earn money, too.

Helping out

Some children are given a bit of money every week by their parents. It is called an allowance. You could also earn money by doing extra jobs around the home.

You could earn money by washing the car.

Selling things

You can collect old toys, clothes, or books that you do not want anymore. You can also make cards, bookmarks, or other things. Then ask an adult to help you to sell all these things on a stand.

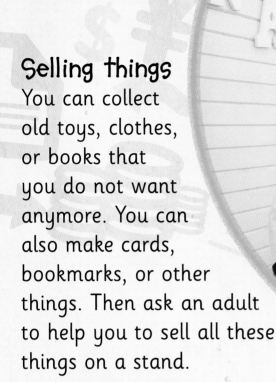

You can earn money by selling thing you have made or things you do not want to keep.

Money talk

Think of a job you could do for money. How much is it fair to charge? Always tell an adult what you want to do, and get their permission.

You can earn money by doing jobs around the home.

SAY WHAT?

There are lots of words and phrases to do with money.

Money words

Some words for money are: cash, green, loot, dough, and bread. A fiver is five dollars. A buck is one dollar.

When someone has millions of dollars of money, such as soccer player David Beckham, we call them a "millionaire."

Long ago, when a group of Roman robbers tried to steal money, some geese made a noise and gave them away. The Romans thought the geese were sent by a goddess called Moneta. We get the word "money" from her name.

The dollar has been around for a long time and there are lots of phrases about dollars:

Sound as a dollar.

Very safe and reliable.

Bet your bottom dollar.

You are certain.

Top dollar.

The best price.

Feel a million dollars.

Feel happy and attractive.

GLOSSARY

account When a bank looks after your money, you have an account with them.

afford When you have enough money to pay for something.

barter Swapping to pay for things without money.

bill Paper money.

budget A plan of how and when to spend money.

change Money you get back when you pay for something.

charity Helping other people.

check A way of paying for things from your bank.

coin Metal object used as money.

cowrie A sea animal with a bright shell.

currency Any kind of money.

decimal Using tens and the numbers 0 to 9.

expenses Money you pay to do something.

income Money you are paid.

minting Making coins.

INDEX

NOTES FOR PARENTS AND TEACHERS

Some children find the concept of value difficult to understand. Practical experience and guidance are the best way to learn about money.

Give your children plenty of practice at finding different ways to make the same value in coins. Start with ways to make 10 cents, then work up to 20 cents, 50 cents and one dollar.

Playing the "store" game is a great way to use coins, and introduces the concept of change. Set problems in different formats.

For example, ask children of how much change would be given for a certain problem. Next time, provide the figure for the change given and ask how much was spent. This will reinforce understanding.

Paper money is harder to understand because the notes tend to be the same size. "Monopoly" bills and other games that use paper money should help a lot.

Managing money

Encourage children to save up for something they want from an early age. The best way to learn budgeting is from experience. It also makes sense to make the link between work and money early on, for example by paying for chores. Remember to keep the jobs age-appropriate.

Creative writing

It can be great fun to tell the story of a coin or a bill. It can have adventures, being used to buy necessities and luxuries, and getting lost or stolen. This all underlines the idea that a coin or bill has a set value throughout its life.